Worship, Praise and Thanksgiving

to

God our defender

Have reverence for the LORD your God
and worship only him.
500 Powerful Warfare Prayers

Apostle Josephine Ujunma Holm

Josephine Ujunma Holm
ISBN: 978-87-93309-12-8
Product of Zion, The City of God.
Website: www.zionthecityofgod.org
Mail: zionthecityofgod@gmail.com
Region Nordjylland, Denmark
 (E-Book) All rights reserved.

Introduction

I have come to understand that biblical worship is all
about telling, communicating, Honouring, applauding,
complimenting, congratulating, paying tribute to God,
giving thanks, blessing, worshiping,cheering God for
who he is in your life and what he means to you and
acknowledging him by saying the Most High God, in
the mighty name of the Lord Jesus Christ, you are the
King of Kings, the Lord of Lords, the Ancient of Days,
The unchangeable Lord, I praise You, Lord, I give you
my offering of thanksgiving, O God, it is right for us to
praise you in Zion and keep our promises to you and I
give you a sacrifice of thanksgiving and offer my prayer
to you, in agreement with 2 Chronicles 29:28 The whole
assembly bowed in worship, while the musicians played
and the trumpets sounded. All this continued until the

sacrifice of the burnt offering was completed, and in 2 Chronicles 20:21-22, [21] After consulting the people, the king appointed singers to walk ahead of the army, singing to the LORD and praising him for his holy splendor. This is what they sang. Give thanks to the LORD; his faithful love endures forever!"[22] At the very moment they began to sing and give praise, the LORD caused the armies of Ammon, Moab, and Mount Seir to start fighting among themselves, for all the congregation worshipped, and the singers sang, and the trumpeters sounded: and all this continued until the burnt offering was finished.

Confession 1
Blessed *be* the LORD my Rock, who trains my hands for war,
And my fingers for battle to kill the enemy, Psalm 144:1

For the weapons of my warfare *are* mighty in God for pulling
down every wicked satanic stronghold of satan in my life to be
destroyed, 2 Corinthians 10:4

 They fought from the heavens; The stars from their courses
fought against Sisera Judges 5:20 The stars of the heavens fight
those who fight against me tonight and every night

So God made **the** two larger lights, **the sun** to rule
over **the** day **and the moon** to rule over **the** night; he also
made **the stars**. Genesis 1:16, **the sun** and **the moon** of the
heavens fight those who fight against me today and every day

O LORD, oppose those who oppose me.
    Fight those who fight against me. Put on your armor, and take
up your shield.
    Prepare for battle, and come to my aid. Lift up your spear and
javelin
    against those who pursue me. Let me hear you say,
    I will give you victory Psalm 35:1-3

Revelation 15:4, Psalm 43

The Lord God of Abraham, Isaac, and **Israel**, my Father, in the

mighty name of the Lord Jesus Christ, with the covenant blood of

the Lord Jesus Christ, I stand in awe of you Lord, to declare your

greatness, as I pray, declare me innocent, and defend me against

Whatever & Whoever among the ungodly satanic agent of the universe on the planet earth, at all times. In the spirit world and the physical world. By the power in the blood of the Lord Jesus Christ, with the authority name of the Lord Jesus Christ. Amen

Revelation 15:4, Psalm 43

The Lord God of Abraham, Isaac, and **Israel**, my Father, in the mighty name of the Lord Jesus Christ with the covenant blood of the Lord Jesus Christ I must praise you Lord, as I pray, deliver me from **Whatever & Whoever among** the evil satanic lying tongues of all wicked, diabolical people of the planet earth at all times. In the spirit world and the physical world. By the power in the blood of the Lord Jesus Christ, with the authority name of the Lord Jesus Christ. Amen

Confession 2

Arise, O LORD, **Rescue** me, my God! Slap all my enemies in the face and Shatter the teeth of the wicked the speak against me today and every day, Psalm 3:7

Return, O LORD, and **rescue** me. Save me because of your unfailing love. Psalm 6:4

I come to you for protection, O LORD my God. Save me from my persecutors—**rescue** me tonight and every night Psalm 7:1

Restore to me the joy of Your salvation, and sustain me with a willing spirit Lord. **Psalm 51:12**

O Lord, open my lips, and my mouth to declare Your praise. **Psalm 51:15 the Lord God deliver** me **out** of the mire, And let me not sink; Let me be **deliver**ed from those who hate me, And **out** of the deep waters. Psalm 69:14

deliver me, O my God, **out** of the hand of the wicked, **Out** of the hand of the unrighteous and cruel man. Psalm 71:4

Revelation 15:4, Psalm 43

 The Lord God of Abraham, Isaac, and **Israel**, my Father, in the mighty name of the Lord Jesus Christ with the covenant blood of the Lord Jesus Christ, I worship You Lord, you are holy and all the nations must come and **worship** you, because your actions are seen by all, as I pray, deliver me from all the cruelty, **brutality**, **spite**, **abuse**, **ill-treatment**, the **harshness** of every wicked one of satan among all my enemies, at all times. In the spirit world and the physical world. By the power in the blood of the Lord Jesus Christ, with the authority name of the Lord Jesus Christ. Amen

1 Corinthians 1:2, Exodus 15:2

The Lord God of Abraham, Isaac, and **Israel**, my Father, in the mighty name of the Lord Jesus Christ with the covenant blood of the Lord Jesus Christ, I **worship** our Lord Jesus Christ, for The LORD is my strong **defend**er; he is the LORD who has saved me. He is my God, and I will praise him, and I will sing about his greatness at all times. In the spirit world and the physical world. By the power in the blood of the Lord Jesus Christ, with the authority name of the Lord Jesus Christ. Amen

Confession 3

the Lord God Stretch **out** Your hand from above; Rescue me and **deliver** me **out** of great waters, From the hand of every wicked satanic foreigner, Psalm 144:7

 the Lord God **deliver** me **out** of all trouble, And my eye has seen *its desire* upon my enemies. Psalm 54:7

"Is this the one who relies on the LORD? Then let the LORD save him! If the LORD loves him so much, let the LORD **rescue** him!" Psalm 22:8

But I trust in your unfailing love Lord. I must rejoice because you have **rescue**d me tonight and every night. Psalm 13:5

Numbers 10:9, Philippians 3:3,
The Lord God of Abraham, Isaac, and **Israel**, my Father, in the mighty name of the Lord Jesus Christ with the covenant blood of the Lord Jesus Christ, I **worship** God, through his Spirit, and I rejoice in my life in union with Christ Jesus, for the LORD my God, help me and save me from the root of **Whatever &**
Whoever among all **the Devil's evil spiritual satanic, diabolical**

traitors, murderers and gang up **of** every wicked, demonic agent of satan among all my enemies, at all times. In the spirit world and the physical world. By the power in the blood of the Lord Jesus Christ, with the authority name of the Lord Jesus Christ. Amen

Deuteronomy 32:4, John 4:24
The Lord God of Abraham, Isaac, and **Israel**, my Father, in the mighty name of the Lord Jesus Christ with the covenant blood of the Lord Jesus Christ, I **worship** you, Lord, for The LORD is my mighty **defend**er, perfect and just in all his ways, my God is faithful and true; he does what is right and fair, at all times. In the spirit world and the physical world. By the power in the blood of the Lord Jesus Christ, with the authority name of the Lord Jesus Christ. Amen

Confession 4

Show me your unfailing love in wonderful ways. By your mighty power Lord Psalm 17:7

Arise, O LORD! Stand against them, and bring them to their
knees! **Rescue** me from the wicked with your sword today and
everyday Psalm 17:13

I love you, LORD; you are my strength today and every day.
Psalm 18:1

The Lord God **rescue** me from my powerful enemies, from those
who hated me today, every day and every night Psalm 18:17

The Lord God, lead me to a place of safety and **rescue** me
because you delight in me. Psalm 18:19

The Lord God **rescue** me from my enemies and hold me safe
beyond the reach of my enemies and save me from violent
opponents. Psalm 18:48

Zechariah 14:9, Deuteronomy 33:29

The Lord God of Abraham, Isaac, and **Israel**, my Father, in the
mighty name of the Lord Jesus Christ with the covenant blood of
the Lord Jesus Christ, I bless you the Holy One of Israel, for
the LORD, will be king over all the earth and everyone must
worship him as God and know him by the same name and
The LORD himself is my shield and my sword, to **defend** me and
give me victory so that all my satanic enemies will come begging
for mercy, and I will destroy them all, at all times. In the spirit
world and the physical world. By the power in the blood of the
Lord Jesus Christ, with the authority name of the Lord Jesus
Christ. Amen

Zechariah 14:21, 1 Samuel 24:15

The Lord God of Abraham, Isaac, and **Israel**, my Father, in the mighty name of the Lord Jesus Christ with the covenant blood of the Lord Jesus Christ, I **worship** the LORD Almighty for The LORD will judge and **defend** me, and save me from the root of **Whatever & Whoever among all the Devil's evil spiritual satanic, diabolical activities** of every wicked satanic person among the witches and wizards at all times. In the spirit world and the physical world. By the power in the blood of the Lord Jesus Christ, with the authority name of the Lord Jesus Christ. Amen

Confession 5

Save me, O God, by Your name, and vindicate me by Your might **Psalm 54:1**

Heal me, O LORD, and I will be healed; save me, and I will be saved, for You are my praise. **Jeremiah 17:14**

Deliver me, O my God, out of every evil satanic hand of the wicked, out of the hand of the unrighteous and cruel man. **Psalm 71:4**

Declare me innocent, O God! **Defend** me against these ungodly people. Rescue me from these unjust liars. For you are God, my only safe haven, Psalm 43

End the evil of those who are wicked against me and **defend** me the righteous. For you look deep within the mind and heart, O righteous God. Psalm 7:9

Micah 4:5, 2 Samuel 22:3

The Lord God of Abraham, Isaac, and **Israel**, my Father, in the mighty name of the Lord Jesus Christ with the covenant blood of the Lord Jesus Christ, I **worship** and obey the LORD our God forever and ever, for My God is my protection, and with him I am safe. He protects me like a shield; he **defend**s me and keeps me safe. He is my savior; he protects me and saves me from every wicked, violent agent of satan at all times. In the spirit world and the physical world. By the power in the blood of the Lord Jesus Christ, with the authority name of the Lord Jesus Christ. Amen

Zechariah 8:22, Micah 5:13, Psalm 18:2

The Lord God of Abraham, Isaac, and **Israel**, my Father, in the mighty name of the Lord Jesus Christ with the covenant blood of the Lord Jesus Christ, I **worship** the LORD Almighty and destroy satanic idols and I kill satanic stone pillars of satan, as I must never **worship** the things that I made by myself, for The

LORD *is* my rock, and my fortress, and my deliverer; my God, my strength, in whom I will trust; my buckler, and the horn of my salvation, *and* my high tower, at all times. In the spirit world and the physical world. By the power in the blood of the Lord Jesus Christ, with the authority name of the Lord Jesus Christ. Amen

2 Samuel 22:47,Job 33:26

The Lord God of Abraham, Isaac, and **Israel**, my Father, in the mighty name of the Lord Jesus Christ with the covenant blood of the Lord Jesus Christ, l **worship you** God with joy, for The LORD, lives and blessed be my Rock, my God, the rock of my salvation, be exalted, at all times. In the spirit world and the physical world. By the power in the blood of the Lord Jesus Christ, with the authority name of the Lord Jesus Christ. Amen

Confession 6

For the angel of the LORD is a guard for me, he surrounds me and **defend**s me who fear the Lord God, Psalm 43:1

Declare me innocent, O God, **Defend** me against these ungodly people. Rescue me from these unjust liars. Psalm 43

Come with great power, O God, and rescue me! **Defend** me with your might, Psalm 54
The Lord God lift me up from every wicked satanic pit of destruction, out of the miry clay and set my feet upon a rock, and

make my footsteps firm. **Psalm 40:2**

Arise, O God, and **defend** my cause. Remember how these fools insult me all day long. Psalm 74:22

psalm 43:4, **2 Samuel 22:47**
 The Lord God of Abraham, Isaac, and **Israel**, my Father, in the mighty name of the Lord Jesus Christ with the covenant blood of the Lord Jesus Christ, I make a joyful noise unto the LORD, I go to your altar, O God; you are the source of my happiness. I play my harp and sing praise to you, O God, my God, for
The LORD lives, praise my **defend**er, Proclaim the greatness of the strong God who saves me, at all times. In the spirit world and the physical world. By the power in the blood of the Lord Jesus Christ, with the authority name of the Lord Jesus Christ. Amen

Psalm 29:2, **2 Samuel 23:12**
The Lord God of Abraham, Isaac, and **Israel**, my Father, in the mighty name of the Lord Jesus Christ with the covenant blood of the Lord Jesus Christ, I honor the LORD for the glory of his name, and I Worship the LORD in the splendor of his holiness, for
The LORD won a great victory for me, at all times. In the spirit world and the physical world. By the power in the blood of the Lord Jesus Christ, with the authority name of the Lord Jesus Christ. Amen

2 Kings 2:12, Psalm 29:2

The Lord God of Abraham, Isaac, and **Israel**, my Father, in the
mighty name of the Lord Jesus Christ with the covenant blood of
the Lord Jesus Christ, I give You all honor Lord, I give unto
the LORD the glory due to His name, and I Worship
the LORD in the beauty of holiness, for The LORD is my
mighty **defend**er, at all times. In the spirit world and the physical
world. By the power in the blood of the Lord Jesus Christ, with
the authority name of the Lord Jesus Christ. Amen

Confession 7

My eyes are always on the LORD, for you Lord God **rescue**s me
from every wicked satanic trap of my enemies. Psalm 25:15

O LORD my God, protect me, **rescue my life, my Spirit, my
Soul, my Body, my mind** from **every wicked satanic secret cult
of the wicked man and woman among my enemy and** do not
let me be disgraced, for in you Lord I take refuge. Psalm 25:20

O LORD my God, protect me, **rescue my life, my Spirit, my
Soul, my Body, my mind** from every wicked evil tongue and
mouth of every wicked person among my enemies, do not let me
be disgraced, for in you Lord I take refuge. Psalm 25:20

I must exalt you, O LORD GOD, for you **rescue** me, You refused
to let my enemies triumph over me today, every day and every
night. Psalm 30:1

Deuteronomy 32:4, **Psalm 100:1-2**

The Lord God of Abraham, Isaac, and **Israel**, my Father, in the mighty name of the Lord Jesus Christ with the covenant blood of the Lord Jesus Christ, I give you Lord all adoration, I Thank you, Lord, I Shout for joy to the LORD, for The LORD is my mighty **defend**er, at all times. In the spirit world and the physical world. By the power in the blood of the Lord Jesus Christ, with the authority name of the Lord Jesus Christ. Amen

Deuteronomy 32:4, **Psalm 100:1-2**

The Lord God of Abraham, Isaac, and **Israel**, my Father, in the mighty name of the Lord Jesus Christ with the covenant blood of the Lord Jesus Christ, I Worship the LORD with gladness for The LORD is my mighty defender, perfect and just in all his ways, at all times. In the spirit world and the physical world. By the power in the blood of the Lord Jesus Christ, with the authority name of the Lord Jesus Christ. Amen

Confession 8

O LORD my God, turn your ear to listen to me; **rescue** me quickly. Be my rock of protection, a fortress where I will be safe. Psalm 31:2

I entrust my spirit into your hand O Lord God. **Rescue** me, LORD, for you are a faithful God. Psalm 31:5

My future is in your hands O Lord God. **Rescue** me from those who hunt me down today, every day and every night Psalm 31:15

Let your favor shine on me O Lord God. In your unfailing love, **rescue** me. Psalm 31:16

Matthew 2:11, Psalm 100:1-2 ,2 Kings 13:14, Judges 5:20
The Lord God of Abraham, Isaac, and **Israel**, my Father, in the mighty name of the Lord Jesus Christ with the covenant blood of the Lord Jesus Christ, I knelt down to **worship** you Lord, You have been the mighty **defend**er of me, let the weapons of the stars *from heaven* utterly **destroy the root of** Whatever & Whoever among **all the Devil's evil spiritual satanic, diabolical** practices

of **every wicked** person of satan man and woman among the satanic neighbors monitoring my life, in my environment, in my **surroundings**, in my **territory** in my **home**, in my city and in my town to die, at all times. In the spirit world and the physical world. By the power in the blood of the Lord Jesus Christ, with the authority name of the Lord Jesus Christ. Amen

Matthew 2:11, Psalm 100:1-2 ,2 Kings 13:14, Judges 5:20
The Lord God of Abraham, Isaac, and **Israel**, my Father, in the mighty name of the Lord Jesus Christ with the covenant blood of the Lord Jesus Christ, I come before you Lord with joyful songs, You have been the mighty **defend**er of me, let the weapons of the stars *from heaven* utterly **destroy** all the works of the devil and all the works of every **wicked** person of Satan man, woman against the works of my hands by the fire, at all times. In the spirit world and the physical world. By the power in the blood of the Lord Jesus Christ, with the authority name of the Lord Jesus Christ. Amen

Confession 9

O Lord God. **Rescue** me, **my life, my Spirit, my Soul, my Body, my mind** from every demonic, satanic attack of the gates of death, plague, and burial and keep me alive even in times of famine. Psalm 33:19

The LORD GOD **rescue** me, **my life, my Spirit, my Soul, my Body, my mind** from all my troubles. Psalm 34:17

I must rejoice in the LORD, and I must be glad because the Lord God **rescue** me from **every wicked satanic occult group, organization, church. among my enemy** Psalm 35:9

The LORD GOD **rescue** me from my rebellion. Do not let fools mock me. Psalm 39:8

Please, LORD GOD, **rescue** me! Come quickly, LORD, and help me. Psalm 40:13

Luke 2:36-37, Psalm 100:1-2,Psalm 4:1

The Lord God of Abraham, Isaac, and **Israel**, my Father, in the mighty name of the Lord Jesus Christ with the covenant blood of the Lord Jesus Christ, I **worship** you God day and night, O God, my **defend**er, be kind to me now and hear my prayer, let the weapons of the stars *from heaven* utterly **destroy all** evil satanic powers of every wicked satanic person among the neighbor flying and walking within and around my family house for evil to die, at all times. In the spirit world and the physical world. By the power in the blood of the Lord Jesus Christ, with the authority name of the Lord Jesus Christ. Amen

Confession 10

The LORD GOD protects me and keeps me alive and gives me prosperity in the land, and **rescues** me from all my enemies today, every day and every night. Psalm 41:2

Declare me innocent, O God! Defend me against those ungodly people, **Rescue** me from those unjust liars today, every day, and every night. Psalm 43:1

The LORD GOD **rescue** me and give me glory Psalm 50:15

Come with great power, O God, and **rescue** me! Defend me with your might today, every day, and every night. Psalm 54:1

For you, Lord God, **rescue** me from my troubles and help me to triumph over every enemy today, every day, and every night. Psalm 54:7

Luke 2:36-37, Psalm 100:1-2,Psalm 4:1, Luke 4:8, Psalm 91:9
The Lord God of Abraham, Isaac, and **Israel**, my Father, in the mighty name of the Lord Jesus Christ with the covenant blood of the Lord Jesus Christ, **I Worship** you the Lord my God, for I have made the LORD my **defend**er, the Most High God my protector, Lord, let the weapons of the stars *from heaven* utterly **destroy the root of Whatever & Whoever among all the Devil's evil spiritual satanic diabolical talisman**, **amulet**, charm, **magic spell**, **enchantment**, the **sorcery** of every **wicked** person of Satan, man, woman that is working against me, my household, **my sons and my daughters** and everything I own for evil to die, at all times. In the spirit world and the physical world.

By the power in the blood of the Lord Jesus Christ, with the authority name of the Lord Jesus Christ. Amen

Confession 11

Vindicate me, O LORD! For I walk with integrity, I trust in the LORD without wavering. **Psalm 26:1**

Vindicate me, my God, and plead my cause against an unfaithful nation. Rescue me from those who are deceitful and wicked. **Psalm 43:1**

Contend with my opponents, O LORD; fight against those who battle me. **Psalm 35:1**

Vindicate me by Your righteousness, O LORD my God, and do not let them gloat over me. **Psalm 35:24**

Judge me, O LORD my God, according to your righteousness; and let them not rejoice over me. **Psalm 35:24**

Plead *my cause*, O LORD, with them that strive with me: fight against them that fight against me. **Psalm 35:1**

Luke 2:36-37, Psalm 100:1-2, Psalm 4:1, Luke 4:8Psalm 81:1 The Lord God of Abraham, Isaac, and **Israel**, my Father, in the mighty name of the Lord Jesus Christ with the covenant blood of the Lord Jesus Christ, **I Worship** you Lord my God, for I Shout for joy to God my **defend**er and sing praise to the Lord God, let the weapons of the stars *from heaven* utterly **destroy root of Whatever & Whoever among all the Devil's evil spiritual satanic diabolical talisman, amulet**, charm, **magic spell, enchantment**, the **sorcery** of every **wicked** person of Satan, man, woman that is working against the foundation of my residence, my house address numbers, my doorpost, for evil to die, at all times. In the spirit world and the physical world. By the power in the blood of the Lord Jesus Christ, with the authority name of the Lord Jesus Christ. Amen

Confession 12

Genesis 25:23
The LORD God**, in the mighty name of the Lord Jesus Christ,** make me to be **stronger** than the others among my enemies tonight, every night, and every day

Joshua 17:13

The LORD God**, in the mighty name of the Lord Jesus Christ, help me** become **stronger**, to drive out every wicked one of satan among my enemies to die tonight, every night, and every day

Judges 1:28
The LORD God**, in the mighty name of the Lord Jesus Christ, help me** become **stronger**, to drive out every wicked strongman of satan among my enemies to die tonight, every night, and every day

Judges 1:28
The LORD God**, in the mighty name of the Lord Jesus Christ, help me** become **stronger**, to drive out every wicked strongwoman of satan among my enemies to die tonight, every night, and every day
Judges 1:28
The LORD God**, in the mighty name of the Lord Jesus Christ, help me** become **stronger**, to drive out every wicked strong person of satan among my enemies to die tonight, every night, and every day

Luke 2:36-37, Psalm 100:1-2,Psalm 4:1, Luke 4:8Psalm 91:2

The Lord God of Abraham, Isaac, and **Israel**, my Father, in the mighty name of the Lord Jesus Christ with the covenant blood of the Lord Jesus Christ, **I Worship** you the Lord my God, for The Lord is my **defend**er and my protector, let the weapons of the stars *from heaven* utterly **destroy the root of Whatever & Whoever among all the Devil's evil spiritual satanic diabolical talisman, amulet**, charm, **magic spell, enchantment**, the **sorcery** of every **wicked** person of Satan, man, woman that is working against the works of my hands, my destiny, my glory, my blessings, my environment, my household, my marriage, my life for evil to die, at all times. In the spirit world and the physical world. By the power in the blood of the Lord Jesus Christ, with the authority name of the Lord Jesus Christ. Amen

Confession 13

Acts 19:20
The LORD God**, in the mighty name of the Lord Jesus Christ,** in this powerful way the word of the Lord keeps spreading and growing **stronger in our Zion the of God church** tonight, every night, and every day

2 Corinthians 7:15
The LORD God**, in the mighty name of the Lord Jesus Christ,** help me grow **stronger** than all those my enemies tonight, every night, and every day

Colossians 2:7
The LORD God**, in the mighty name of the Lord Jesus Christ,** help me to keep my roots deep in God, to build my life on God, and to become **stronger** in my faith tonight, every night, and every day

James 4:6

But the grace that God gives me is even **stronger**. As the scripture says, God give me the grace to be humble to him tonight, every night, and every day
Psalm 99:5, Psalm 18:2

The Lord God of Abraham, Isaac, and **Israel**, my Father, in the mighty name of the Lord Jesus Christ with the covenant blood of the Lord Jesus Christ, I Praise the LORD our God and **worship** before his Holy throne, for the LORD is my protector; he is my strong fortress. Let the weapons of the stars *from heaven* utterly **destroy the root of Whatever & Whoever among all the Devil's evil spiritual satanic, diabolical** *blood covenant, blood sacrifice, Bloodsucking demons, switch doctor* of every wicked, diabolical agent of satan and every **wicked** person of Satan, man, woman that is working against my human body internal blood organ systems my spirit, my soul my body for evil to die, at all times. In the spirit world and the physical world. By the power in the blood of the Lord Jesus Christ, with the authority name of the Lord Jesus Christ. Amen

2 Maccabees 1:3, Psalm 18:2, Jonah 1:9
The Lord God of Abraham, Isaac, and **Israel**, my Father, in the mighty name of the Lord Jesus Christ with the covenant blood of the Lord Jesus Christ, I **worship** the LORD, the God of heaven, who made land and sea for My God is my protection, and with him I am safe. Let the weapons of the stars *from heaven* utterly **destroy the root of Whatever & Whoever among all the Devil's evil spiritual satanic diabolical** *Vampire blood-sucking demons, links, pots, ungodly covenants, assignments, ceremonies, gods, shrines and idols, the ungodly dedication* that is working

against *my head, my hands, my legs, and my organs,* for evil to die, at all times. In the spirit world and the physical world. By the power in the blood of the Lord Jesus Christ, with the authority name of the Lord Jesus Christ. Amen

Confession 14

Judges 3:12
The LORD God**, in the mighty name of the Lord Jesus Christ, help to** overpower every wicked one of satan among my enemies tonight, every night, and every day
Daniel 1:15
The LORD God**, in the mighty name of the Lord Jesus Christ, help me to** healthier and **stronger** than all those my enemies tonight, every night, and every day

Judges 3:12
The LORD God**, in the mighty name of the Lord Jesus Christ, help me to** overpower every wicked king of satan among my enemies tonight, every night, and every day

Judges 3:12
The LORD God**, in the mighty name of the Lord Jesus Christ, help me to** overpower every wicked queen of satan among my enemies tonight, every night, and every day

Daniel 11:5

The LORD God, **in the mighty name of the Lord Jesus Christ, help me to** be even **stronger** and rule a greater kingdom than all those my enemies tonight, every night, and every day

 Daniel 11:23
The LORD God, **in the mighty name of the Lord Jesus Christ, help me to** grow **stronger** and **stronger** than all those my enemies tonight, every night, and every day

2 Maccabees 1:3, Psalm 18:2, Zechariah 8:21
The Lord God of Abraham, Isaac, and **Israel**, my Father, in the mighty name of the Lord Jesus Christ with the covenant blood of the Lord Jesus Christ

I am going to **worship** the LORD Almighty and pray for his Blessing

for my God is my protection, and with him, I am safe. Let the weapons of the stars *from heaven* utterly **destroy root of Whatever & Whoever among all the Devil's evil spiritual satanic, diabolical** *ancestral covenant, satanic boyfriends and satanic girlfriends,* witches and wizards that are working against *my laughter, my joy, my helpers* for evil to die, at all times. In the spirit world and the physical world. By the power in the blood of the Lord Jesus Christ, with the authority name of the Lord Jesus Christ. Amen

Confession 15

But I will call on God, and the LORD will **rescue** me. Psalm 55:16

For you the Lord God have **rescue**d me from death; you have kept my feet from slipping. So now I can walk in your presence, O God, in your life-giving light. Psalm 56:13

The Lord God send help from heaven to **rescue** me, disgracing those who hound me. Interlude My God will send forth his unfailing love and faithfulness, Psalm 57:3

Rescue me from my enemies, O God. Protect me from those who have come to destroy me. Psalm 59:1

Rescue me from these criminals; save me from these murderers. Psalm 59:2

You are my strength; I wait for you to **rescue** me, for you, O God, are my fortress. Psalm 59:9

Rescue me from the mud; don't let me sink any deeper! Save me from those who hate me, and pull me from these deep waters. Psalm 69:14

Job 4:6, Psalm 28:1

The Lord God of Abraham, Isaac, and **Israel**, my Father, in the mighty name of the Lord Jesus Christ with the covenant blood of the Lord Jesus Christ, I **worship** you God, and my life is blameless. So, I have confidence and hope in you Lord my **defend**er, I call to you. Listen to my cry Almighty God, let the weapons of the stars *from heaven* utterly **destroy the root of**

Whatever & Whoever among all the Devil's evil spiritual satanic diabolical satellite technologies of **every wicked person of satan and every wicked one of satan that is working against me,** at all times. In the spirit world and the physical world. By the power in the blood of the Lord Jesus Christ, with the authority name of the Lord Jesus Christ. Amen

Psalm 16:4, Psalm 35:23, Daniel 3:14
The Lord God of Abraham, Isaac, and Israel, my Father, in the mighty name of the Lord Jesus Christ with the covenant blood of the Lord Jesus Christ, I worship the Almighty GOD of Shadrach, Meshach, and Abednego **for Those who rush to satanic gods, bring many troubles on themselves. I will not take part in their diabolical sacrifices; I will not worship their satanic gods as I pray O Lord defend me; rise up, my God, and plead my cause. Almighty God, let the weapons of the stars** *from heaven* **utterly destroy the root of Whatever & Whoever among all the Devil's evil spiritual satanic diabolical satellite communications of every wicked person of satan and every wicked one of satan that is working against me** to die, at all times. In the spirit world and the physical world. By the power in the blood of the Lord Jesus Christ, with the authority name of the Lord Jesus Christ. Amen

Confession 16

Please, God, **rescue** me. Come quickly, LORD, and help me.
Psalm 70:1

Save me and **rescue** me, for you do what is right. Turn your ear to
listen to me, and set me free Lord Psalm 71:2

My God, **rescue** me from the power of the wicked and from the
clutches of cruel oppressors. Psalm 71:4

the LORD my God **rescue** me from every wicked satanic land of
satan and as I open my mouth wide, and fill it with good things
Lord. Psalm 81:10

the LORD my God, Your love for me is so great that you protect
me from death and the grave Psalm 86:13

the LORD my God, **rescue** me from every trap of satan and protect
me from the deadly disease of satan Psalm 91:3

The LORD God **rescue** me who love you and protect me who trust
in your name. Psalm 91:14

Remember me, LORD, when you show favor to your people; come
near and **rescue** me. Psalm 106:4

Luke 24:52, Psalm 18:1

The Lord God of Abraham, Isaac, and **Israel**, my Father, in the

mighty name of the Lord Jesus Christ with the covenant blood of

the Lord Jesus Christ, I **worship** you Lord as I am filled with great joy, I love you, LORD my **defend**er, let the weapons of the stars *from heaven* utterly **destroy the root of Whatever & Whoever among all the Devil's evil spiritual satanic, diabolical** enchantment, **bewitchment** magical spell, **witchcraft, voodoo, wizardry, sorcery, occultism, incantation, necromancy** occult forces and evil spirits of every **wicked** person of Satan, man, woman that is working against me, my home, my properties, my legs and everything I do for evil to die, at all times. In the spirit world and the physical world. By the power in the blood of the Lord Jesus Christ, with the authority name of the Lord Jesus Christ. Amen

Psalm 22:23, Psalm 43:1
The Lord God of Abraham, Isaac, and Israel, my Father, in the mighty name of the Lord Jesus Christ with the covenant blood of the Lord Jesus Christ, I Worship and honor you LORD, declare me innocent, and defend my cause against the ungodly and deliver me from all lying tongues of evil wicked satanic people, Almighty God, let the weapons of the stars *from heaven* **utterly destroy the root of Whatever & Whoever among all the Devil's evil spiritual satanic diabolical satellite networks of every wicked person of satan and every wicked one of satan that are working against me** to die, at all times. In the spirit world and the physical world. By the power in the blood of the Lord Jesus Christ, with the authority name of the Lord Jesus Christ. Amen

Jeremiah 7:1-3, Psalm 1:1–4

The Lord God of Abraham, Isaac, and Israel, my Father, in the mighty name of the Lord Jesus Christ with the covenant blood of the Lord Jesus Christ,

I **worship** the LORD Almighty, the God of Israel, for I reject the advice of evil satanic people, and I do not follow the example of satanic sinners, and I will never join those wicked satanic people who have no use for God. Instead, I find joy in obeying the Law of the LORD,

and I study it day and night, so I am   like trees that grow beside a stream,

That bear fruit at the right time, and my leaves do not dry up. I succeed in everything they do today and every day. But evil, wicked satanic people among my enemies are not like this at all; they are like straw that the wind blows away out of my life, at all times. In the spirit world and the physical world. By the power in the blood of the Lord Jesus Christ, with the authority name of the Lord Jesus Christ. Amen

Confession 16

O Sovereign LORD, for the sake of your own
reputation! **Rescue** me because you are so faithful and good.
Psalm 109:21

Rescue me, O LORD, from liars and from all deceitful people.
Psalm 120:2

O LORD, **rescue** me from evil people. Protect me from those who
are violent, Psalm 140:1

O Sovereign LORD, the strong one who **rescue**d me, protect me
on the day of battle. Psalm 140:7

Rescue me from my persecutors, for they are too strong for me.
Psalm 142:6

Rescue me from my enemies, LORD; I run to you to hide me.
Psalm 143:9

Isaiah 48:1, Psalm 35:5
**The Lord God of Abraham, Isaac, and Israel, my Father, in
the mighty name of the Lord Jesus Christ with the covenant
blood of the Lord Jesus Christ,**

I **worship** the God of Israel; I **worship** you Lord, with all my
heart, and

May **Whatever & Whoever among all the Devil's evil spiritual
satanic diabolical criminal minds and criminal activities of,
the wicked man the wicked woman, the wicked person** and

The wicked, diabolical agent of satan among **my enemies** be like
chaff before the wind, with the angel of the LORD driving them
away from me forever, at all times. In the spirit world and the

physical world. By the power in the blood of the Lord Jesus Christ, with the authority name of the Lord Jesus Christ. Amen

Psalm 59:17, Psalm 35:5
The Lord God of Abraham, Isaac, and Israel, my Father, in the mighty name of the Lord Jesus Christ with the covenant blood of the Lord Jesus Christ,

I must praise you Lord, my **defend**er. My refuge is God, the God who loves me, and May **Whatever & Whoever among all the Devil's evil spiritual satanic diabolical criminal minds and criminal activities of, the wicked man the wicked woman, the wicked person** and The wicked, diabolical agent of satan among **my enemies** be like chaff before the wind, with the angel of the LORD driving them away from me forever, at all times. In the spirit world and the physical world. By the power in the blood of the Lord Jesus Christ, with the authority name of the Lord Jesus Christ. Amen

Psalm 62:2, Psalm 99:9, Psalm 35:5
The Lord God of Abraham, Isaac, and Israel, my Father, in the mighty name of the Lord Jesus Christ with the covenant blood of the Lord Jesus Christ,

I Praise the LORD our God, and I **worship** at his sacred hill, for The LORD our God is holy, and The Lord alone protects me and saves me; he is my **defend**er, and I shall never be defeated, and May all my satanic enemies be like chaff before the wind, with the angel of the LORD driving them away from me today, every day and every night, at all times. In the spirit world and the physical world. By the power in the blood of the Lord Jesus Christ, with the authority name of the Lord Jesus Christ. Amen

Confession 18

Reach down from heaven and **rescue** me; **rescue** me from deep waters, from the power of my enemies. Psalm 144:7

Save me! **Rescue** me from the power of my enemies. Their mouths are full of lies; they swear to tell the truth, but they lie instead. Psalm 144:11

You brought me up from the grave, O LORD. You kept me from falling into the pit of **death**. Psalm 145:19

For you have rescued me from **death** and have kept my feet from slipping. So now I can walk in your presence, O God, in your life-giving light. Psalm 56:13

The Sovereign LORD rescue me from **death**. Psalm 68:20

Psalm 100:2, Psalm 37:38

The Lord God of Abraham, Isaac, and Israel, my Father, in the mighty name of the Lord Jesus Christ with the covenant blood of the Lord Jesus Christ, I **worship** the Lord, the Almighty, the Most High God, for the Lord God who rescues me and protects me is like a mighty rock, and all satanic sinners among my enemies will be destroyed, and there will be no future for the wicked enemy that works against me today, every day and every night, at all times. In the spirit world and the physical world. By the power in the blood of the Lord Jesus Christ, with the authority name of the Lord Jesus Christ. Amen

Psalm 102:22, Psalm 105:4, Isaiah 37:36

The Lord God of Abraham, Isaac, and Israel, my Father, in the mighty name of the Lord Jesus Christ with the covenant blood of the Lord Jesus Christ, I Worship the LORD with joy, and I come before him with happy songs, for I Go to the LORD for help. I **worship** him continually, for An angel of the LORD go into every satanic camp of all my adversaries to kill 185,000 of my enemies today, every day and every night, at all times. In the spirit world and the physical world. By the power in the blood of the Lord Jesus Christ, with the authority name of the Lord Jesus Christ. Amen

Confession 19

None of us can see our own errors; **deliver** me, LORD, from
hidden faults
Psalm 19:12

O God, declare me innocent, and defend my cause against the
ungodly; **deliver** me from lying and evil people! Psalm 43:1

LORD, waiting for you to save me, I place my trust in your word.
Psalm 89:46
  Psalm 119:123

With all my heart, I call to you; answer me, LORD, and I must
obey your commands! Psalm 119:145

The LORD God be a **refuge** for me in times of trouble. Psalm 9:9

The LORD God *is* my strength Psalm 28:8

Bow down Your ear to me, deliver me speedily; Be my rock
of **refuge**, A fortress of defense to save me, Lord. Psalm 31:2

Psalm 115:11, Psalm 143:12
**The Lord God of Abraham, Isaac, and Israel, my Father, in
the mighty name of the Lord Jesus Christ with the covenant
blood of the Lord Jesus Christ,** I trust in the LORD, I
worship the Lord God and He helps me and protects me, And in
Your lovingkindness, cut off my enemies And destroy all those
who afflict my soul, at all times. In the spirit world and the
physical world. By the power in the blood of the Lord Jesus
Christ, with the authority name of the Lord Jesus Christ. Amen

Proverbs 28:5,Psalm 135:20,Psalm 52:5

The Lord God of Abraham, Isaac, and Israel, my Father, in the mighty name of the Lord Jesus Christ with the covenant blood of the Lord Jesus Christ, I Praise the LORD GOD, FOR Surely God will bring every wicked one of satan among all my oppressors, my **persecutor**s, my **tormentor**s down to everlasting ruin; He will snatch them up and tear them away from their tent; and He will uproot Every wicked one of satan among my oppressors, my **persecutor**s, my **tormentor**s, from the land of the living, at all times. In the spirit world and the physical world. By the power in the blood of the Lord Jesus Christ, with the authority name of the Lord Jesus Christ. Amen

Confession 20

The LORD of hosts *is* with me; Psalm 46:7

The Lord God *is* in my palaces; He is known as my **refuge**. Psalm 48:3

Be merciful to me, O God, be merciful to me! For my soul trusts in You; And in the shadow of Your wings I make my **refuge**, until *all satanic* calamities have passed by. Psalm 57:1

The Lord God I must sing of Your power; Yes, I must sing aloud of Your mercy in the morning; For You have been my defense and **refuge** in the day of my trouble. Psalm 59:16

In God *is* my salvation and my glory; The rock of my strength, *and* my **refuge**, *is* in God. Psalm 62:7

 I Trust in Lord at all times for God *is* a **refuge** for me, Psalm 62:8

Psalm 33:8, Psalm 40:4, Psalm 42:2, Isaiah 29:5
The Lord God of Abraham, Isaac, and Israel, my Father, in the mighty name of the Lord Jesus Christ with the covenant blood of the Lord Jesus Christ, I Worship the LORD MY GOD, I trust the LORD, I thirst for you, the living God, I **worship** in your presence Lord, for the multitude of every wicked one of satan among all my oppressors, my **persecutor**s, my **tormentor**s shall become like fine dust. It shall happen instantly, suddenly, at all times. In the spirit world and the physical world. By the power in the blood of the Lord Jesus Christ, with the authority name of the Lord Jesus Christ. Amen

Psalm 50:1 Isaiah 29:5
The Lord God of Abraham, Isaac, and Israel, my Father, in the mighty name of the Lord Jesus Christ with the covenant blood of the Lord Jesus Christ, I *genuinely **Worship*** the Almighty God, And the multitude of every wicked person of satan all my oppressors shall become like the chaff which blows away. It shall happen instantly, suddenly, at all times. In the spirit world and the physical world. By the power in the blood of the Lord Jesus Christ, with the authority name of the Lord Jesus Christ. Amen

Confession 21

The Lord God be my strong **refuge,** For You *are* my rock and my fortress. Psalm 71:3

I must say of the Lord, *He is* my **refuge** and my fortress; My God, in Him I must trust. Psalm 91:2

Because I have made the Lord God, *who is* my **refuge**, *Even* the Most High, my dwelling place, Psalm 91:9

O Lord God, to whom vengeance belongs, O God, to whom vengeance belongs, shine forth to help me Psalm 94:1

But the Lord God has been my defense, and my God is the rock of my **refuge**. Psalm 94:22

But my eyes *are* upon You, O Lord God, In You I take **refuge** Psalm 141:8

I cried out to You, O Lord: I said, "You *are* my **refuge**, My portion in the land of the living. Psalm 142:5

My lovingkindness and my fortress, my high tower and my deliverer, My shield and *the One* in whom I take **refuge**, Who subdues the wicked satanic people under me. Psalm 144:2

Psalm 66:4, Isaiah 54:15

**The Lord God of Abraham, Isaac, and Israel, my Father, in
the mighty name of the Lord Jesus Christ with the covenant
blood of the Lord Jesus Christ,** I **worship** you, Lord, I sing
praises to you, Lord, for Behold, they shall surely gather together,
but not by God. Whosoever shall gather together against me shall
fall for my sake, at all times. In the spirit world and the physical
world. By the power in the blood of the Lord Jesus Christ, with
the authority name of the Lord Jesus Christ. Amen

Psalm 69:6, Psalm 2:9

**The Lord God of Abraham, Isaac, and Israel, my Father, in
the mighty name of the Lord Jesus Christ with the covenant
blood of the Lord Jesus Christ,** I **worship** you, O God of Israel,
I sing praises to your name Lord, for The Lord shall break every
wicked one of satan among all my oppressors, my **persecutor**s,
my **tormentor**s with a rod of iron and dash them to pieces like a
potter's vessel, at all times. In the spirit world and the physical
world. By the power in the blood of the Lord Jesus Christ, with
the authority name of the Lord Jesus Christ. Amen

Confession 22

The LORD GOD is my rock and my fortress and my deliverer; My
God, my **strength**, in whom I will trust; My shield and the horn
of my salvation, my stronghold. Psalm 18:2

It is God who arms me with **strength**, and makes my way perfect.
Psalm 18:32

For You have armed me with **strength** for the battle; You have
subdued under me those who rose up against me. Psalm 18:39

Let the words of my mouth and the meditation of my heart Be
acceptable in Your sight, O LORD, my **strength** and my
Redeemer. Psalm 19:14

May the Lord God send me help from the sanctuary,
and **strength**en me in **Zion**, the City of God, Psalm 20:2

The LORD GOD is great and is to be highly praised in the city of
our God, on his sacred hill. Psalm 48:1

Psalm 89:15,1 Samuel 2:10

**The Lord God of Abraham, Isaac, and Israel, my Father, in
the mighty name of the Lord Jesus Christ with the covenant
blood of the Lord Jesus Christ,** I **worship** you Lord with songs,
and I live in the light of your kindness Lord, for Those who
oppose the LORD will be shattered. He will thunder from heaven
against them, at all times. In the spirit world and the physical
world. By the power in the blood of the Lord Jesus Christ, with
the authority name of the Lord Jesus Christ. Amen

Psalm 95:6, Psalm 89:23

**The Lord God of Abraham, Isaac, and Israel, my Father, in
the mighty name of the Lord Jesus Christ with the covenant
blood of the Lord Jesus Christ,** I bow down to

worship Sovereign LORD Almighty, and I kneel before the LORD, our Maker, for the Lord God will beat down my adversaries before me, and strike those who hate me. at all times. In the spirit world and the physical world. By the power in the blood of the Lord Jesus Christ, with the authority name of the Lord Jesus Christ. Amen

Confession 24

The LORD God *is* my **strength**, Psalm 28:8

 Give unto the LORD GOD, O you mighty ones, Give unto the LORD glory and **strength**. Psalm 29:1

The LORD GOD give **strength** to me and His people, The LORD GOD bless me and His people with peace Psalm 29:11

Pull me out of the net which they have secretly laid for me, For You *are* my **strength Lord**. Psalm 31:4

I Be of good courage for the Lord God **strength**en my heart, as I hope in the LORD. Psalm 31:24

The LORD GOD **strength**en me out of every wicked satanic bed of illness for The LORD GOD **empower** me out of every wicked satanic sickbed. Psalm 41:3

For You *are* the God of my **strength**; Why do You cast me off? Why do I go mourning because of the oppression of the enemy? Psalm 43:2

God *is* my refuge and **strength**, A very present help in trouble.
Psalm 46:1

2 Corinthians 10:4, **Psalm 18:46**

The Lord God of Abraham, Isaac, and **Israel**, my Father, in the
mighty name of the Lord Jesus Christ with the covenant blood of
the Lord Jesus Christ, I Praise the Lord, my **defend**er, and I
Proclaim the greatness of the God who saves me, for the weapons
of my warfare are mighty through God to destroy all types of
satanic enemies **among all my** oppressors to die, at all times. In
the spirit world and the physical world. By the power in the blood
of the Lord Jesus Christ, with the authority name of the Lord
Jesus Christ. Amen

Jonah 1:9, Psalm 34:16

The Lord God of Abraham, Isaac, and **Israel**, my Father, in the
mighty name of the Lord Jesus Christ with the covenant blood of
the Lord Jesus Christ, I **worship** the LORD, the God of heaven,
who made land and sea, for The face **of** the Lord *is* against those
diabolical enemies who do evil against me to **cut off** the
remembrance **of** them from the earth, at all times. In the spirit
world and the physical world. By the power in the blood of the
Lord Jesus Christ, with the authority name of the Lord Jesus
Christ. Amen

Confession 25

Save me, O God, by Your name, and vindicate me by
Your **strength**. Psalm 54:1

I must wait for You Lord my **Strength**; For God *is* my defense.
Psalm 59:9

To You, O Lord God my **Strength**, I must sing praises; For
God *is* my defense, My God of mercy. Psalm 59:17

In God *is* my salvation and my glory; The rock of
my **strength**, *and* my refuge, *is* in God. Psalm 62:7

O Lord God, *you are* more awesome than Your holy places. The
Lord God of Israel gives me **strength** and power Blessed *be* God!
Psalm 68:35

O Lord God do not cast me off in the time of old age and do not
forsake me, don't my **strength** fail at all times Psalm 71:9

I go into the **strength** of the Lord GOD and I make mention of
Your righteousness Lord God Psalm 71:16

Psalm 55:22.Psalm 59:17
The Lord God of Abraham, Isaac, and **Israel**, my Father, in the
mighty name of the Lord Jesus Christ with the covenant blood of
the Lord Jesus Christ,

I must praise you, my **defend**er. My refuge is God, the God who loves me and

I Leave my troubles with the LORD, and the Lord will **defend** me, and he never let me be defeated. at all times. In the spirit world and the physical world. By the power in the blood of the Lord Jesus Christ, with the authority name of the Lord Jesus Christ. Amen

Nehemiah 8:6, Psalm 37:9

The Lord God of Abraham, Isaac, and **Israel**, my Father, in the mighty name of the Lord Jesus Christ with the covenant blood of the Lord Jesus Christ, I Praise and **worship** the LORD, the great God, For every wicked one of satan among the evildoers against me shall be **cut off**, shall be **cut off**, shall be **cut off**, at all times. In the spirit world and the physical world. By the power in the blood of the Lord Jesus Christ, with the authority name of the Lord Jesus Christ. Amen

Confession 26

O Lord God, do not forsake me at all times, Psalm 71:18

But the Lord God *is* the **strength** of my heart and my portion forever. Psalm 73:26

I Sing aloud to God my **strength** and I Make a joyful shout to the Lord God. Psalm 81:1

The Lord God help me to go from **strength** to **strength** Psalm 84:7

Oh Lord God, turn to me, and have mercy on me! Give Your **strength** to me Psalm 86:16

Honor and majesty *are* before God and **Strength** and beauty *are* in His sanctuary, Psalm 96:6

The Lord God *is* my **strength** and song, And He has become my salvation. Psalm 118:14

Exodus 15:2, Psalm 2:9 The Lord God of Abraham, Isaac, and **Israel**, my Father, in the mighty name of the Lord Jesus Christ with the covenant blood of the Lord Jesus Christ, The Lord is my strength and my song; he has given me victory, This is my God, and I will praise Him and I will exalt him! for the Lord break Whatever & Whoever among all the power of my enemy with a rod of iron and smash them like clay pots, at all times. In the spirit world and the physical world. By the power in the blood of the Lord Jesus Christ, with the authority name of the Lord Jesus Christ. Amen

Confession 27

Arise, O Lord, to Your resting place, You and the ark of Your **strength**. Psalm 132:8

O God the Lord, the **strength** of my salvation, cover my head in the day of battle. Psalm 140:7

The LORD GOD is my protector, my **strong** fortress, my protection, and with him I am safe. God protects me like a shield; he defends me and keeps me safe. Psalm 18:2

God rescue me from my powerful enemies and from all those who hate me Psalm 18:17

the Lord God who make me **strong** and make my pathway safe at all times. Psalm 18:32

the Lord God train me for battle, so that I can use the **strong**est bow to destroy my enemies at all times. Psalm 18:34

the LORD MY GOD, **strong** and mighty, the LORD is victorious in all my battle at all times. Psalm 24:8

Deuteronomy 32:3

The Lord God of Abraham, Isaac, and **Israel**, my Father, in the mighty name of the Lord Jesus Christ with the covenant blood of the Lord Jesus Christ, I must proclaim the name of the LORD; how glorious is our God for the LORD break root of Whatever & Whoever among **all the Devil's evil spiritual satanic, diabolical movements and wickedness of the wicked man and the wicked woman, the wicked person and the** wicked, diabolical agent of satan **that want to** steal, kill and destroy from me with a rod of iron, He breaks them in pieces like a clay pot, at all times. In the spirit world and the physical world. By the power in the blood of the Lord Jesus Christ, with the authority name of the Lord Jesus Christ. Amen

Judges 5:3, 2 Chronicles 33:16,1 Samuel 2:10, Exodus 15:6
The Lord God of Abraham, Isaac, and **Israel**, my Father, in the mighty name of the Lord Jesus Christ with the covenant blood of the Lord Jesus Christ,

 I **worship** the LORD, the God of Israel, Listen, you kings, pay attention, you mighty rulers, For I will sing to the LORD, I must make music to the LORD, the God of Israel, for Those who oppose the LORD will be shattered. The LORD thunder from heaven against them and Your right hand, O LORD, is majestic in power; Your right hand, O LORD, has shattered my enemy, at all times. In the spirit world and the physical world. By the power in the blood of the Lord Jesus Christ, with the authority name of the Lord Jesus Christ. Amen

2 Samuel 22:1-3, 2 Chronicles 6:7, Exodus 15:6

The Lord God of Abraham, Isaac, and **Israel**, my Father, in the mighty name of the Lord Jesus Christ with the covenant blood of the Lord Jesus Christ, I **worship** the LORD of God of Israel,
The LORD is my rock, my fortress, and my savior; my God is my rock, in whom I find protection. He is my shield, the power that saves me, and my place of safety, He is my refuge, my savior, the one who saves me from all my enemies, and Your right hand, O LORD, is glorious in power. Your right hand, O LORD, smashes Whatever & Whoever among my enemy to die, at all times. In the spirit world and the physical world. By the power in the blood of the Lord Jesus Christ, with the authority name of the Lord Jesus Christ. Amen

Confession 28

I be **strong**, I be courageous as I put all my hope in the LORD.
Psalm 31:24

With all my heart I must say to the LORD GOD, there is no one like
you. You protect me from the **strong** oppressor at all time Psalm
35:10

for you the Lord God are my protector, my **strong** defense against
my enemies at all times. Psalm 61:3

My salvation and my honor depend on the Lord God for he is
my **strong** protector; he is my shelter at all times Psalm 62:7

Be my secure shelter and a **strong** fortress to protect me Lord
God, you are my refuge and defense at all times. Psalm 71:3

My life has been an example to many, because you Lord God
have been my **strong** defender at all times. Psalm 71:7

Make me **strong** again, and we, your people, will praise you
LORD GOD at all times . Psalm 85:6

2 Samuel 22:4, Nehemiah 9:3. Psalm 3:7

The Lord God of Abraham, Isaac, and **Israel**, my Father, in the
mighty name of the Lord Jesus Christ with the covenant blood of
the Lord Jesus Christ, I **worship** you LORD my God, I called on
the LORD, who is worthy of my praise, and he saved me from my
enemies and Lord, rise up! My God, save me! You, Lord, have
struck my enemies on the cheek, and Lord, you have broken the

teeth of my wicked enemy to be destroyed, at all times. In the spirit world and the physical world. By the power in the blood of the Lord Jesus Christ, with the authority name of the Lord Jesus Christ. Amen

2 Samuel 22:47, 2 Chronicles 30:8, Psalm 3:7

The Lord God of Abraham, Isaac, and **Israel**, my Father, in the mighty name of the Lord Jesus Christ with the covenant blood of the Lord Jesus Christ, I do not be stubborn, I obey the LORD, and I **worship** the LORD, my God so that he will no longer be angry with me. The LORD lives, Praise to my Rock, May God, the Rock of my salvation, be exalted and Lord, rise up! My God, save me, and Lord, strike all my enemies in the face, and the Lord breaks the teeth of the wicked, sinful satanic people among my enemies to be destroyed at all times. In the spirit world and the physical world. By the power in the blood of the Lord Jesus Christ, with the authority name of the Lord Jesus Christ. Amen

2 Samuel 22:50, Nehemiah 9:5,2 Chronicles 15:15,

The Lord God of Abraham, Isaac, and **Israel**, my Father, in the mighty name of the Lord Jesus Christ with the covenant blood of the Lord Jesus Christ, I Stand up to praise the LORD my God forever and ever! Let everyone praise his glorious name, For this, O LORD, I will praise you among the nations; I will sing praises to your name. at all times. In the spirit world and the physical world.

By the power in the blood of the Lord Jesus Christ, with the authority name of the Lord Jesus Christ. Amen

1 Chronicles 16:8 and Psalm 91:10

The Lord God of Abraham, Isaac, and **Israel**, my Father, in the mighty name of the Lord Jesus Christ with the covenant blood of the Lord Jesus Christ, I delight in **worship**ing the LORD. I Give thanks to the LORD and proclaim his greatness and Let the whole world know what he has done and no harm will overtake me, no disaster will come near my tent, and I say again, *no evil shall be allowed to befall me, no plague will come near my tent*, at all times. In the spirit world and the physical world. By the power in the blood of the Lord Jesus Christ, with the authority name of the Lord Jesus Christ. Amen

1 Chronicles 16:92 Chronicles 24:18, Psalm 91:10

The Lord God of Abraham, Isaac, and **Israel**, my Father, in the mighty name of the Lord Jesus Christ with the covenant blood of the Lord Jesus Christ, I keep **worship**ing in the Temple of the LORD, the God of Israel and I Sing to the Lord; yes, I sing his praises. And I tell everyone about his wonderful deeds and no evil will conquer me; no plague will come near my home and I say again, *no harm will overtake me, no disaster will come near my* *tent,* at all times. In the spirit world and the physical world. By the power in the blood of the Lord Jesus Christ, with the authority name of the Lord Jesus Christ. Amen

Confession 29

The strength of the Lord God must always be with me for the power of the Lord God make me **strong at all times** . Psalm 89:21

Lord God You have made me as **strong** as a wild ox; you have blessed me with happiness at all times Psalm 92:10

I stay young and **strong** like an eagle. Psalm 103:5

Praise the LORD, you **strong** and mighty angels, who obey his commands, who listen to what he says. Psalm 103:20

The LORD GOD makes me powerful and **strong**; he has saved me at all times. Psalm 118:14

My Sovereign LORD, my **strong** defender, you have protected me in every satanic battle at all times. Psalm 140:7

Listen to my cry for help Lord, Save me from my enemies at all times Psalm 142:6

1 Chronicles 16:34,2 Chronicles 6:10, Psalm 91:10

The Lord God of Abraham, Isaac, and **Israel**, my Father, in the mighty name of the Lord Jesus Christ with the covenant blood of the Lord Jesus Christ,

I **worship** of the LORD God of Israel, and I Give thanks to

the LORD, for he is good and His faithful love endures forever. No

evil shall be allowed to befall me, no plague come near my home,

and I say again, *no satanic evil shall be entitled to befall me, no*

satanic plague will come near my household, at all times. In the

spirit world and the physical world. By the power in the blood of

the Lord Jesus Christ, with the authority name of the Lord Jesus

Christ. Amen

1 Chronicles 16:35, 2 Chronicles 7:3, Psalm 91:10

The Lord God of Abraham, Isaac, and **Israel**, my Father, in the mighty name of the Lord Jesus Christ with the covenant blood of the Lord Jesus Christ, I keep **worship**ing God and praising him for his goodness and his eternal love. And we Cry out, Save us, O God of our salvation and Gather and rescue us from among the nations, so we can thank your holy name and rejoice and praise you Lord, and no terrible satanic disasters will strike me or my home, and I say again, *no satanic evil will conquer me; no satanic plague will come near my home* at all times. In the spirit world and the physical world. By the power in the blood of the Lord Jesus Christ, with the authority name of the Lord Jesus Christ. Amen

1 Chronicles 16:36,1 Chronicles 16:11, Psalm 91:10

The Lord God of Abraham, Isaac, and **Israel**, my Father, in the mighty name of the Lord Jesus Christ with the covenant blood of the Lord Jesus Christ,

I Go to the LORD for help, and I **worship** the LORD continually, and I praise the LORD, the God of Israel, who lives from everlasting to everlasting, and all the people shout "Amen!" and praised the LORD, and no evil satanic will befall me, no satanic plague will approach my house, I say again, *No satanic evil shall befall me, No satanic plague will come near my dwelling* at all times. In the spirit world and the physical world. By the power in the blood of the Lord Jesus Christ, with the authority name of the Lord Jesus Christ. Amen

Come to Confession 30

the Lord God keep my gates **strong**; he blesses the people that love me Psalm 147:13

the Lord God put his angels in charge of me to protect me wherever I go at all times **Psalm 91:11**

For it is written: the Lord God command His angels concerning me to guard me carefully at all timed **Luke 4:10**

For the lord God will command His angels concerning me to guard me in all my ways at all times **Psalm 91:11**

O Lord God Stop the **wickedness** of evildoers and reward me and those who are good. **Psalm 7:9**

Come and save me, LORD; in your mercy **rescue** me from all terrible things of *all Human Wickedness* Psalm 6:4

O LORD, my God, I come to you for protection; **rescue** me and save me from all terrible satanic things of *all Human Wickedness*, Psalm 7:1

Be merciful to me, O LORD! See the sufferings my enemies cause me! **Rescue** me from death, O LORD, Psalm 9:13

I rely on your constant love; I will be glad, because you will **rescue** me. Psalm 13:5

O Lord God destroy them for their satanic **wickedness** and destroy them for their sins for the LORD our God destroy enemies at all times. **Psalm 94:23**

O Lord God Keep me from wanting to do wrong and from joining evil people in their satanic **wickedness**. May I never take part in their feasts. **Psalm 141:4**

O Lord God make every wicked one of satan among enemies to pay for their **wickedness Jeremiah 14:16**

O LORD, don't stay away from me! Come quickly to my **rescue** from all kinds of satanic **wickedness**, evil, greed, jealousy, murder, fighting, deceit, and malice, gossip Psalm 22:19

O LORD God remove all satanic **wickedness** from me and from the descendants of me

O LORD God rescue me from all satanic **wickedness at all times**

1 Peter 2:9,2 Chronicles 11:16, Psalm 91:10

The Lord God of Abraham, Isaac, and **Israel**, my Father, in the mighty name of the Lord Jesus Christ with the covenant blood of the Lord Jesus Christ, I **worship** the LORD, the God of Israel, and I sing songs of thanks and praise to the Lord God, and so no satanic disaster will strike me, no violence will come near my home and I say again, no harm will come to me; no satanic plague will come near my house, at all times. In the spirit world and the physical world. By the power in the blood of the Lord Jesus Christ, with the authority name of the Lord Jesus Christ. Amen

1 Peter 4:11, Psalm 91:10

The Lord God of Abraham, Isaac, and **Israel**, my Father, in the mighty name of the Lord Jesus Christ with the covenant blood of the Lord Jesus Christ, All praise to God, the Father of our Lord Jesus Christ. It is by his great mercy that I have been born again because God raised Jesus Christ from the dead. Now I live with great expectation, and no evil will fall upon me, and no satanic affliction will approach my house, and I say again,

No satanic evil will overtake me; no satanic illness will come near my home. at all times. In the spirit world and the physical world.

By the power in the blood of the Lord Jesus Christ, with the authority name of the Lord Jesus Christ. Amen

Jude 1:24-25, Psalm 91:10

The Lord God of Abraham, Isaac, and **Israel**, my Father, in the mighty name of the Lord Jesus Christ with the covenant blood of the Lord Jesus Christ, Now all glory to God, who is able to keep me from falling away and will bring me with great joy into his glorious presence without a single fault. [25] All glory to him who alone is God, our Savior through Jesus Christ, our Lord. All glory, majesty, power, and authority are his before all time, and in the present, and beyond all time! Amen and no satanic evil shall overtake me, and no satanic plague shall come near my dwelling and I say again, satanic evil shall not come near me, and satanic disease shall not come near my dwellings, at all times. In the spirit world and the physical world. By the power in the blood of the Lord Jesus Christ, with the authority name of the Lord Jesus Christ. Amen

Revelation 5:13, Psalm 91:10

The Lord God of Abraham, Isaac, and **Israel**, my Father, in the mighty name of the Lord Jesus Christ with the covenant blood of the Lord Jesus Christ, I say Blessing and honor and glory and power belong to the Lord God sitting on the throne and to the Lamb forever and ever. No harm will come to me, and No satanic sickness will come near my house, and There shall no evil befall me, and no satanic plague will come near my dwelling, at all times. In the spirit world and the physical world. By the power in the blood of the Lord Jesus Christ, with the authority name of the Lord Jesus Christ. Amen

Revelation 7:12, Psalm 91:10 -11

The Lord God of Abraham, Isaac, and **Israel**, my Father, in the mighty name of the Lord Jesus Christ with the covenant blood of the Lord Jesus Christ, I say Blessing and glory and wisdom and thanksgiving and honor and power and strength belong to our God forever and ever! Amen, and no satanic evil will conquer me, and no satanic plague will come near my home, For the Lord God order his angels to protect me wherever I go today and every day and every night at all times. In the spirit world and the physical world. By the power in the blood of the Lord Jesus Christ, with the authority name of the Lord Jesus Christ. Amen

Revelation 19:1, Psalm 91:10 -11

The Lord God of Abraham, Isaac, and **Israel**, my Father, in the mighty name of the Lord Jesus Christ with the covenant blood of the Lord Jesus Christ, I say Praise the LORD for Salvation and glory and power belong to our God. No satanic evil shall befall me, and No satanic plague will come near my dwelling, For the Lord God give His angels charge over me, To keep me in all my ways today and every day and every night at all times. In the spirit world and the physical world. By the power in the blood of the Lord Jesus Christ, with the authority name of the Lord Jesus Christ. Amen

Revelation 19:5, Psalm 91:10 -11

The Lord God of Abraham, Isaac, and **Israel**, my Father, in the mighty name of the Lord Jesus Christ with the covenant blood of the Lord Jesus Christ, I say praise our God, all his servants, all who fear him, from the least to the greatest and There shall no satanic evil befall me, no satanic plague *and* calamity will come near my tent, For the Lord God give His angels charge over me to accompany me *and* to defend me *and* preserve me in all my ways of obedience and service today and every day and every night at all times. In the spirit world and the physical world. By the power in the blood of the Lord Jesus Christ, with the authority name of the Lord Jesus Christ. Amen

Colossians 1:3-4, Numbers 14:12

The Lord God of Abraham, Isaac, and **Israel**, my Father, in the mighty name of the Lord Jesus Christ with the covenant blood of the Lord Jesus Christ, I give thanks to God, the Father of our Lord Jesus Christ, and the Lord God strike every wicked satanic person among witches and wizards in the camp of my enemies down with a plague and destroy them, and the Lord God make me into a nation greater and stronger than all my wicked satanic enemies in the universe, at all times. In the spirit world and the physical world. By the power in the blood of the Lord Jesus Christ, with the authority name of the Lord Jesus Christ. Amen

Colossians 2:6-7, Job 5:19
The Lord God of Abraham, Isaac, and **Israel**, my Father, in the mighty name of the Lord Jesus Christ with the covenant blood of the Lord Jesus Christ, As I have received Christ Jesus the Lord, *so* I walk in Christ Jesus: rooted and built up in Christ Jesus, and established in the faith, as I have been taught, abounding therein with thanksgiving and the Lord God rescue me from six satanic calamities; no harm will touch me in seven. at all times. In the spirit world and the physical world. By the power in the blood of the Lord Jesus Christ, with the authority name of the Lord Jesus Christ. Amen

Colossians 3:15, Job 5:19

The Lord God of Abraham, Isaac, and **Israel**, my Father, in the mighty name of the Lord Jesus Christ with the covenant blood of the Lord Jesus Christ, let the peace of God rule in my heart and my body. I be thankful for the Lord God set me free From six satanic calamities and he will rescue me, so in seven no harm will touch me, at all times. In the spirit world and the physical world. By the power in the blood of the Lord Jesus Christ, with the authority name of the Lord Jesus Christ. Amen

Colossians 4:2, Job 5:19

 The Lord God of Abraham, Isaac, and **Israel**, my Father, in the mighty name of the Lord Jesus Christ with the covenant blood of the Lord Jesus Christ, **I** continue in prayer and watch in the same with thanksgiving to the Lord, and the Lord God rescue me from six satanic calamities, and no harm will touch me in seven, at all times. In the spirit world and the physical world. By the power in the blood of the Lord Jesus Christ, with the authority name of the Lord Jesus Christ. Amen

1 Thessalonians 5:16-18,

The Lord God of Abraham, Isaac, and **Israel**, my Father, in the mighty name of the Lord Jesus Christ with the covenant blood of the Lord Jesus Christ, I rejoice evermore, and I Pray without ceasing, and In everything, I give thanks to the LORD God, for this is the will of God in Christ Jesus concerning me, and in **Psalm 121:7** The LORD preserve me from all satanic evil, and he shall preserve my soul, and in **Job 5:19** The LORD set me free From six satanic disasters, and He will rescue me; even in the seventh, he keeps me free from all satanic evil, at all times. In the spirit world and the physical world. By the power in the blood of the Lord Jesus Christ, with the authority name of the Lord Jesus Christ. Amen

1 Thessalonians 5:23-24

 The Lord God of Abraham, Isaac, and **Israel**, my Father, in the mighty name of the Lord Jesus Christ with the covenant blood of the Lord Jesus Christ, I keep **worship**ing you Lord with all my heart, and the very God of peace sanctify me wholly; and *I pray God* my whole spirit and soul and body be preserved blameless unto the coming of our Lord Jesus Christ for. Faithful *is* he that calleth me, who also will do *it*, and in **Job 5:19** The Lord God deliver me from six satanic troubles; in seven no evil shall touch me today and every day and every night, at all times. In the spirit world and the physical world. By the power in the blood of the Lord Jesus Christ, with the authority name of the Lord Jesus Christ. Amen

2 Thessalonians 1:11, 1 Chronicles 16:4

The Lord God of Abraham, Isaac, and **Israel**, my Father, in the
mighty name of the Lord Jesus Christ with the covenant blood of
the Lord Jesus Christ, I **worship** of the LORD, the God of Israel,
by singing and praising him, I always pray for me, that our God
counts me worthy of *this* calling and fulfill all the good pleasure
of *his* goodness, and the work of faith with power. In **Psalm
34:19,** the LORD God delivers me from all the wicked afflictions
of satan and his cohorts, at all times. In the spirit world and the
physical world. By the power in the blood of the Lord Jesus
Christ, with the authority name of the Lord Jesus Christ. Amen

2 Thessalonians 3:3, Psalm 16:7

The Lord God of Abraham, Isaac, and **Israel**, my Father, in the
mighty name of the Lord Jesus Christ with the covenant blood of
the Lord Jesus Christ, I bless the LORD who guides me; even at
night my heart instructs The Lord and me is faithful, he shall
establish me, and keep *me* from all satanic evil of every enemy, at
all times. In the spirit world and the physical world. By the power
in the blood of the Lord Jesus Christ, with the authority name of
the Lord Jesus Christ. Amen

2 Thessalonians 3:5, Psalm 13:6, Psalm 5:11, Psalm 91:10

The Lord God of Abraham, Isaac, and **Israel**, my Father, in the mighty name of the Lord Jesus Christ with the covenant blood of the Lord Jesus Christ, I sing joyful praises to the Lord God forever and I must sing to the LORD because he is good to me and the Lord direct my heart into the love of God, and into the patient waiting for Christ for no satanic evil organizer shall overtake me, and no evil satanic intentions shall come near my dwelling, at all times. In the spirit world and the physical world. By the power in the blood of the Lord Jesus Christ, with the authority name of the Lord Jesus Christ. Amen

1 Timothy 1:17, Psalm 7:17, Psalm91:10

The Lord God of Abraham, Isaac, and **Israel**, my Father, in the mighty name of the Lord Jesus Christ with the covenant blood of the Lord Jesus Christ, I must thank the LORD because he is just; I must sing praise to the name of the LORD Most High. Now unto the King eternal, immortal, invisible, the only wise God, *be* honour and glory for ever and ever. Amen for no satanic evil **Wickedness** shall happen to me and no **wicked** agent of satan will come near my dwelling. at all times. In the spirit world and the physical world. By the power in the blood of the Lord Jesus Christ, with the authority name of the Lord Jesus Christ. Amen

1 Timothy 4:4-5, Psalm 9:1-2,

The Lord God of Abraham, Isaac, and **Israel**, my Father, in the mighty name of the Lord Jesus Christ with the covenant blood of the Lord Jesus Christ, I must praise you, LORD, with all my heart;   I must tell of all the marvelous things you have done for me, I must be filled with joy because of you Lord. I must sing praises to your name, O Most High God, and in **Psalm 91:10** No satanic evil of the wicked man and woman will overtake me and satanic no illness will come near my home, at all times. In the spirit world and the physical world. By the power in the blood of the Lord Jesus Christ, with the authority name of the Lord Jesus Christ. Amen

Hebrews 13:15, 2 Chronicles 20:21,
The Lord God of Abraham, Isaac, and **Israel**, my Father, in the mighty name of the Lord Jesus Christ with the covenant blood of the Lord Jesus Christ, **I** give thanks to the LORD for your faithful love endures forever. I offer the sacrifice of praise to God continually, that is, the fruit of *my* lips giving thanks to his name, and in **Psalm 91:10,** no satanic evil of the wicked person will befall me and no satanic evil plague will approach my household, at all times. In the spirit world and the physical world. By the power in the blood of the Lord Jesus Christ, with the authority name of the Lord Jesus Christ. Amen

1 Chronicles 29:10, Psalm 9:11, Psalm 91:10

The Lord God of Abraham, Isaac, and **Israel**, my Father, in the mighty name of the Lord Jesus Christ with the covenant blood of the Lord Jesus Christ, **I** Sing praises to the LORD who reigns in Jerusalem and tell the world about his extraordinary deeds for me and Evil satanic **spirit of madness and insanity** shall not come near me, and satanic disease shall not come near my dwellings, at all times. In the spirit world and the physical world. By the power in the blood of the Lord Jesus Christ, with the authority name of the Lord Jesus Christ. Amen

1 Chronicles 29:13

The Lord God of Abraham, Isaac, and **Israel**, my Father, in the mighty name of the Lord Jesus Christ with the covenant blood of the Lord Jesus Christ, Now, therefore, our God, we thank you Lord and praise your glorious name. In **Psalm 91:10,** No evil, wicked satanic person among **murderers** shall befall me, and No evil, wicked satanic man and woman among **killers will** come near my dwelling, at all times. In the spirit world and the physical world. By the power in the blood of the Lord Jesus Christ, with the authority name of the Lord Jesus Christ. Amen

Psalm 18:3, Psalm 91:10

The Lord God of Abraham, Isaac, and **Israel**, my Father, in the mighty name of the Lord Jesus Christ with the covenant blood of the Lord Jesus Christ, I called on the LORD, who is worthy of my praise, and he saved me from my enemies and no evil, the wicked satanic **criminal** person **among all the kidnappers and evil Plotters** shall be allowed to befall me and no evil, wicked satanic **criminal** man and woman **among all the kidnappers and evil Plotters** will come near my household, at all times. In the spirit world and the physical world. By the power in the blood of the Lord Jesus Christ, with the authority name of the Lord Jesus Christ. Amen

Psalm 18:49, Psalm 91:10

The Lord God of Abraham, Isaac, and **Israel**, my Father, in the mighty name of the Lord Jesus Christ with the covenant blood of the Lord Jesus Christ, I must praise you O Lord among the nations, I must sing praises to your name Lord, and no evil, the wicked satanic **criminal** person **among** all the **Ritualists** and **armed robbers** will conquer me and no evil, wicked satanic **criminal** man and woman **among** all the **Ritualists,** and **armed robbers** will come near my home, at all times. In the spirit world and the physical world. By the power in the blood of the Lord Jesus Christ, with the authority name of the Lord Jesus Christ. Amen

Psalm 101:1

The Lord God of Abraham, Isaac, and **Israel**, my Father, in the mighty name of the Lord Jesus Christ with the covenant blood of the Lord Jesus Christ, I must sing of Your loving devotion and justice; to You, O LORD, I will sing praise and in **Psalm 51:14** Deliver me from the guilt of bloodshed, O God, you are my Savior, and my tongue will sing of your righteousness and in **Psalm 26:9** Lord, Do not take my soul away with sinners and do not take my life away with men of bloodshed, at all times. In the spirit world and the physical world. By the power in the blood of the Lord Jesus Christ, with the authority name of the Lord Jesus Christ. Amen

Psalm 138:5

The Lord God of Abraham, Isaac, and **Israel**, my Father, in the mighty name of the Lord Jesus Christ with the covenant blood of the Lord Jesus Christ,

l sing of the ways of the LORD, for the glory of the LORD is great and in **Psalm 25:5**

Guide me in Your truth and teach me, for You are the God of my salvation and in **Psalm 39:8**

Lord Deliver me from all my transgressions and do not make me the reproach of fools at all times. In the spirit world and the physical world. By the power in the blood of the Lord Jesus Christ, with the authority name of the Lord Jesus Christ. Amen

Psalm 28:6, Psalm 23:5

The Lord God of Abraham, Isaac, and **Israel**, my Father, in the mighty name of the Lord Jesus Christ with the covenant blood of the Lord Jesus Christ, I praise the LORD, For he has heard my cry for mercy and the Lord God prepare a table before me in the presence of my enemies for the Lord anoint my head with oil; my cup overflows, and in **Psalm 35:28** my tongue must proclaim Your righteousness Lord and Your praises all day long, at all times. In the spirit world and the physical world. By the power in the blood of the Lord Jesus Christ, with the authority name of the Lord Jesus Christ. Amen

Psalm 29:2, Psalm 27:13

The Lord God of Abraham, Isaac, and **Israel**, my Father, in the mighty name of the Lord Jesus Christ with the covenant blood of the Lord Jesus Christ, I Honor the LORD for the glory of his name, and I Worship the LORD in the splendor of his holiness for I see the goodness of the LORD in the land of the living and in **Psalm 71:16,** I enter into the strength of the Lord GOD, and I will proclaim Your righteousness Lord --Yours alone, at all times. In the spirit world and the physical world. By the power in the blood of the Lord Jesus Christ, with the authority name of the Lord Jesus Christ. Amen

Psalm 32:11, Psalm 145:7

The Lord God of Abraham, Isaac, and **Israel**, my Father, in the mighty name of the Lord Jesus Christ with the covenant blood of the Lord Jesus Christ, So I rejoice in the LORD and be glad, I say Shout for joy, all you whose hearts are pure and I celebrate your abundant goodness Lord and I joyfully sing of your righteousness and in **Psalm 51:14** deliver me from bloodguilt, O God, the God of my salvation. My tongue will sing of Your righteousness at all times. In the spirit world and the physical world. By the power in the blood of the Lord Jesus Christ, with the authority name of the Lord Jesus Christ. Amen

Psalm 86:12-13 The Lord God of Abraham, Isaac, and **Israel**, my Father, in the mighty name of the Lord Jesus Christ with the covenant blood of the Lord Jesus Christ, With all my heart I must praise you, O Lord my God and I must give glory to your name forever, for your love for me is very great. You, Lord, have rescued me from every way that leads to death, at all times. In the spirit world and the physical world. By the power in the blood of the Lord Jesus Christ, with the authority name of the Lord Jesus Christ. Amen

Psalm 34:1 The Lord God of Abraham, Isaac, and **Israel**, my Father, in the mighty name of the Lord Jesus Christ with the covenant blood of the Lord Jesus Christ, I must praise the LORD at all times and I must constantly speak your praises Lord and in **Psalm 6:4** Turn, O LORD, and deliver my soul; save me because of Your loving devotion and in **Psalm 17:13** Arise, O LORD, confront my enemies and bring them to their knees and deliver me from the wicked by Your sword, at all times. In the spirit world and the physical world. By the power in the blood of the Lord Jesus Christ, with the authority name of the Lord Jesus Christ. Amen

Psalm 35:18, The Lord God of Abraham, Isaac, and **Israel**, my Father, in the mighty name of the Lord Jesus Christ with the covenant blood of the Lord Jesus Christ, I must thank you Lord in front of the great assembly, and I must praise you Lord before all the people and in **Psalm 3:7** Arise, LORD! Deliver me, my God! Strike all my enemies on the jaw; break the teeth of the wicked person speak against me and in **Psalm 7:6,** Arise, O LORD, in Your anger; rise up against the fury of my enemies. Awake, my God, and ordain judgment. at all times. In the spirit world and the physical world. By the power in the blood of the Lord Jesus Christ, with the authority name of the Lord Jesus Christ. Amen

Psalm 47:6 The Lord God of Abraham, Isaac, and **Israel**, my Father, in the mighty name of the Lord Jesus Christ with the covenant blood of the Lord Jesus Christ, I Sing praises to God, I Sing praises to our King the Lord GOD and in **Exodus 15:6** Your right hand, LORD, is majestic in power. Your right hand, O LORD, shattered the enemy in my life, and in **Psalm 18:48,** the Lord God delivers me from my enemies and the Lord exalt me above my foes and the Lord rescue me from violent satanic men, at all times. In the spirit world and the physical world. By the

power in the blood of the Lord Jesus Christ, with the authority
name of the Lord Jesus Christ. Amen

Psalm 48:1, The Lord God of Abraham, Isaac, and **Israel**, my
Father, in the mighty name of the Lord Jesus Christ with the
covenant blood of the Lord Jesus Christ, Great *is* the LORD, and
greatly to be praised for In the city of our God, *In* His holy
mountain and in **Numbers 23:23** For there is no satanic
enchantment against me and no satanic divination against me;
now it shall be said of me 'What has God wrought! And in **Psalm
3:7,** Arise, O LORD! Deliver me, O my God! Strike all my
enemies on the jaw; break the teeth of the wicked person that is
speaking satanic evil against me at all times. In the spirit world
and the physical world. By the power in the blood of the Lord
Jesus Christ, with the authority name of the Lord Jesus Christ.
Amen

Psalm 50:14, The Lord God of Abraham, Isaac, and **Israel**, my
Father, in the mighty name of the Lord Jesus Christ with the
covenant blood of the Lord Jesus Christ, I Offer to God
thanksgiving and in **Psalm 5:10** destroy every wicked one of

satan among my enemies, O God; let all my enemies fall by their own counsels; cast them out in the multitude of their transgressions; for they have rebelled against you, at all times. In the spirit world and the physical world. By the power in the blood of the Lord Jesus Christ, with the authority name of the Lord Jesus Christ. Amen

Luke 19:37-38,

The Lord God of Abraham, Isaac, and **Israel**, my Father, in the mighty name of the Lord Jesus Christ with the covenant blood of the Lord Jesus Christ, I rejoice and praise God with a loud voice for all the mighty works we are seen, and we are saying:" 'Blessed *is* the King who comes in the name of the LORD, Peace in heaven and glory in the highest and in **PSALMS 5:10,** Destroy every wicked one of satan among all my enemies, O God; let all my enemies fall by their own counsels; cast them out in the multitude of their transgressions; for they have rebelled against you at all times. In the spirit world and the physical world. By the power in the blood of the Lord Jesus Christ, with the authority name of the Lord Jesus Christ. Amen

Ephesians 1:3

The Lord God of Abraham, Isaac, and **Israel**, my Father, in the mighty name of the Lord Jesus Christ with the covenant blood of the Lord Jesus Christ, Blessed *be* the Lord God and Father of our Lord Jesus Christ, who has blessed me with every spiritual blessing in the heavenly *places* in Christ, and in **Exodus 15:6** Your right hand, LORD, is majestic in power. Your right hand, LORD, break in pieces the enemy in my life and Your right hand, O LORD, glorious in power, your right hand, O LORD, break in pieces every wicked one of satan among all my enemies at all times. In the spirit world and the physical world, By the power in the blood of the Lord Jesus Christ, with the authority name of the Lord Jesus Christ. Amen

Romans 15:11, Ephesians 5:19-20.

The Lord God of Abraham, Isaac, and **Israel**, my Father, in the mighty name of the Lord Jesus Christ with the covenant blood of the Lord Jesus Christ, we are speaking to one another in psalms and hymns and spiritual songs, singing and making melody in our hearts to the Lord, giving thanks always for all things to God the Father in the name of our Lord Jesus Christ, and in **Exodus 15:6** your right hand, O Lord Jehovah God, is become glorious in power: Thy right hand, O Lord Jehovah God

put to death Whatever & Whoever among **all the Devil's evil spiritual satanic, diabolical movements and wickedness of the wicked powers, the wicked kingdoms, the wicked person, the wicked man and the wicked woman that come to** steal, kill and destroy from me **to die, to die** in the camp of the enemy, at all times. In the spirit world and the physical world. By the power in the blood of the Lord Jesus Christ, with the authority name of the Lord Jesus Christ. Amen

Revelation 19:6

The Lord God of Abraham, Isaac, and **Israel**, my Father, in the mighty name of the Lord Jesus Christ with the covenant blood of the Lord Jesus Christ, I **Praise** God! For the Lord, our Almighty God is King, and in **Exodus 15:6** your right hand, O Lord Jehovah God, is become glorious in power: Thy right hand, O Lord Jehovah God **put to death** Whatever & Whoever among **all the Devil's evil spiritual satanic, diabolical movements and wickedness of** wicked, diabolical agent of satan **that come to** steal, kill and destroy from me **to die, to die** in the camp of the enemy at all times. In the spirit world and the physical world. By the power in the blood of the Lord Jesus Christ, with the authority name of the Lord Jesus Christ. Amen

Ephesians 1:6

The Lord God of Abraham, Isaac, and **Israel**, my Father, in the mighty name of the Lord Jesus Christ with the covenant blood of the Lord Jesus Christ, let us **praise** God for his glorious grace, for the free gift he gave us in his dear Son and in **Psalm 145:7** I must extol the fame of Your abundant goodness and joyfully sing of Your righteousness O Lord and in **Psalm 69:23** Let the eyes of Whatever & Whoever among **the wicked satanic person, satanic man, and woman** among **my enemies** be darkened so that they cannot see me. Their backs are bent forever, and in **Psalm 6:10,** May all my enemies are disgraced and terrified. May they suddenly turn back in shame, at all times. In the spirit world and the physical world. By the power in the blood of the Lord Jesus Christ, with the authority name of the Lord Jesus Christ. Amen

Philippians 4:8

The Lord God of Abraham, Isaac, and **Israel**, my Father, in the mighty name of the Lord Jesus Christ with the covenant blood of the Lord Jesus Christ, I must sing **praise**s to you Lord and, In conclusion, my friends, l my mind with those things that are good and that deserve **praise**: things that are true, noble, right, pure, lovely, and honorable and in **Psalm 5:10,** Pronounce **Whatever & Whoever among all the Devil's evil spiritual satanic diabolical occultic powers and occultic kingdoms of the wicked person, the wicked man and the sinful woman among all my enemies** guilty, O God, let them fall by their own counsels, Cast them out in the multitude of their transgressions,

For they have rebelled against You, at all times. In the spirit world and the physical world. By the power in the blood of the Lord Jesus Christ, with the authority name of the Lord Jesus Christ. Amen

Hebrews 13:15

The Lord God of Abraham, Isaac, and **Israel**, my Father, in the mighty name of the Lord Jesus Christ with the covenant blood of the Lord Jesus Christ, Let me always offer **praise** to God as my sacrifice through Jesus, which is the offering presented by my lips that confess him as Lord and in **Psalm 7:6,** Arise, O LORD GOD, in Your anger; Lift Yourself up because of the rage of my enemies, Rise up for me *to* the judgment You have commanded and in **Psalm 71:13,** Let them be confounded *and* consumed Who are adversaries of my life, let them be covered *with* reproach and dishonor Who seek my hurt, at all times. In the spirit world and the physical world. By the power in the blood of the Lord Jesus Christ, with the authority name of the Lord Jesus Christ. Amen

Ephesians 1:12

The Lord God of Abraham, Isaac, and **Israel**, my Father, in the mighty name of the Lord Jesus Christ with the covenant blood of the Lord Jesus Christ, let us, who are the first to hope in Christ, **praise** God's glory and in **Psalm 71:24** My tongue must talk of Your righteousness all the day long Lord, For they are confounded Who seek my hurt., for they are brought to shame

Who seek my hurt and in **Romans 8:1,** So now there is no condemnation, **blame**, **accusation**, negative constructions for me who belong to Christ Jesus at all times. In the spirit world and the physical world. By the power in the blood of the Lord Jesus Christ, with the authority name of the Lord Jesus Christ. Amen

Ephesians 5:19

The Lord God of Abraham, Isaac, and **Israel**, my Father, in the mighty name of the Lord Jesus Christ with the covenant blood of the Lord Jesus Christ, We Must Speak to one another with the words of psalms, hymns, and sacred songs; we sing hymns and psalms to the Lord with **praise** in our hearts and in **Colossians 1:13** For the Lord God has rescued me from every wicked dominion of Lucifer, the devil and brought me into the kingdom of the Son he loves and in **Romans 8:1** Therefore, there is now no condemnation **blame**, **accusation**, negative constructions for me in Christ Jesus, at all times. In the spirit world and the physical world. By the power in the blood of the Lord Jesus Christ, with the authority name of the Lord Jesus Christ. Amen

Daniel 2:20

The Lord God of Abraham, Isaac, and **Israel**, my Father, in the mighty name of the Lord Jesus Christ with the covenant blood of the Lord Jesus Christ, God is wise and powerful, I **Praise** him forever and ever and **in Psalm 57:1**Have mercy on me, my God, have mercy on me, for in you I take refuge. I must take refuge in the shadow of your wings until the disaster has passed, and in Psalm 37:9For wicked satanic evildoers among my enemies shall

be **cut** off, at all times. In the spirit world and the physical world.
By the power in the blood of the Lord Jesus Christ, with the
authority name of the Lord Jesus Christ. Amen

Daniel 2:23

The Lord God of Abraham, Isaac, and **Israel**, my Father, in the
mighty name of the Lord Jesus Christ with the covenant blood of
the Lord Jesus Christ, I **praise** you LORD and honor you, for You
have given me wisdom and strength Lord and in **Psalm 57:1**
Have mercy on me, O God, have mercy, I look to you LORD for
protection. I must hide beneath the shadow of your wings until the
danger passes by now and forever and in **Psalm 57:1**
Be merciful to me, O God, be merciful to me, for in you my soul
takes refuge; in the shadow of your wings, I must take refuge, till
the storms of destruction pass by now and forever at all times. In
the spirit world and the physical world. By the power in the blood
of the Lord Jesus Christ, with the authority name of the Lord
Jesus Christ. Amen

Jeremiah 51:15

The Lord God of Abraham, Isaac, and **Israel**, my Father, in the mighty name of the Lord Jesus Christ with the covenant blood of the Lord Jesus Christ, I say, *a Hymn of **Praise** to God for*
The LORD made the earth by his power, by his wisdom he created the world and stretched out the heavens and in **Psalm 62:2** The Lord alone protects me and saves me; he is my **defend**er, and I must never be defeated now and forever and in **Psalm 6:10** Let all mine enemies be ashamed now and forever at all times. In the spirit world and the physical world. By the power in the blood of the Lord Jesus Christ, with the authority name of the Lord Jesus Christ. Amen

Joel 2:26
The Lord God of Abraham, Isaac, and **Israel**, my Father, in the mighty name of the Lord Jesus Christ with the covenant blood of the Lord Jesus Christ, l **praise** the LORD my God, who has done wonderful things for me, so I and the people of my household will never be despised again and in **Psalm 6:10** let My enemies know the bitter shame of defeat; in sudden confusion, they will be driven away and in **Psalm 7:6** Rise in your anger, O LORD! Stand up against the fury of my enemies; rouse yourself and help me! Justice is what you demand at all times. In the spirit world and the physical world. By the power in the blood of the Lord Jesus Christ, with the authority name of the Lord Jesus Christ. Amen

Jonah 2:9

The Lord God of Abraham, Isaac, and **Israel**, my Father, in the mighty name of the Lord Jesus Christ with the covenant blood of the Lord Jesus Christ, I must sing **praise**s to you Lord, I must offer you a sacrifice and do what I have promised. Salvation comes from the LORD and in **Psalm 35:23** Awake and rise to my defense, to my cause, my God and my Lord and in **Psalm 71:3** Be my rock of refuge, where I can always go. Give the command to save me, Lord, for You are my rock and my fortress, at all times. In the spirit world and the physical world. By the power in the blood of the Lord Jesus Christ, with the authority name of the Lord Jesus Christ. Amen

Romans 16:25

The Lord God of Abraham, Isaac, and **Israel**, my Father, in the mighty name of the Lord Jesus Christ with the covenant blood of the Lord Jesus Christ, let us give glory to God! He is able to make me stand firm in my faith, according to the Good News I preach about Jesus Christ and according to the revelation of the secret truth which was hidden for long ages in the past and in **Psalm 94:1** O LORD God, to whom vengeance belongs; O God, to whom vengeance belongs, show yourself and in **Psalm 7:9** O

LORD God let the wickedness of the wicked come to an end at all times. In the spirit world and the physical world. By the power in the blood of the Lord Jesus Christ, with the authority name of the Lord Jesus Christ. Amen

Romans 15:9

The Lord God of Abraham, Isaac, and **Israel**, my Father, in the mighty name of the Lord Jesus Christ with the covenant blood of the Lord Jesus Christ, I must sing **praise**s to God and in **Psalm 7:9** let the wickedness of the wicked come to an end at all times. In the spirit world and the physical world. By the power in the blood of the Lord Jesus Christ, with the authority name of the Lord Jesus Christ. Amen

Romans 15:6

The Lord God of Abraham, Isaac, and **Israel**, my Father, in the mighty name of the Lord Jesus Christ with the covenant blood of the Lord Jesus Christ, so that all of us together may **praise** with one voice the God and Father of our Lord Jesus Christ, at all times. In the spirit world and the physical world. By the power in the blood of the Lord Jesus Christ, with the authority name of the Lord Jesus Christ. Amen

Philippians 1:11

The Lord God of Abraham, Isaac, and **Israel**, my Father, in the mighty name of the Lord Jesus Christ with the covenant blood of the Lord Jesus Christ, my life must be filled with the truly good qualities which only Jesus Christ can produce, for the glory and **praise** of God, at all times. In the spirit world and the physical world. By the power in the blood of the Lord Jesus Christ, with the authority name of the Lord Jesus Christ. Amen

Exodus 15:2, The Lord is my strength, my song, and my salvation.
He is my God, and I will praise him.
He is my father's God—I will exalt him.

Deuteronomy 32:3, I will proclaim the greatness of the Lord. How glorious he is!

Judges 5:3, Listen, O you kings and princes,For I shall sing about the Lord, The God of Israel.

2 Samuel 22:1-3, David sang this song to the Lord after he had rescued him from Saul and from all his other enemies: [2] Jehovah is my rock, My fortress and my savior.
[3] I will hide in God, Who is my rock and my refuge. He is my shield And my salvation, My refuge and high tower. Thank you, O my Savior, For saving me from all my enemies.

2 Samuel 22:4, I will call upon the Lord, Who is worthy to be praised;
He will save me from all my enemies.

2 Samuel 22:47, The Lord lives. Blessed be my Rock. Praise to him—
The Rock of my salvation.

2 Samuel 22:50, No wonder I give thanks to you, O Lord, among the nations,
And sing praises to your name.

1 Kings 8:56, Blessed be the Lord who has fulfilled his promise and given rest to his people Israel; not one word has failed of all the wonderful promises proclaimed by his servant Moses.

2 Samuel 22:4, I will call upon the Lord, Who is worthy to be praised;
He will save me from all my enemies.

2 Samuel 22:47, The Lord lives. Blessed be my Rock. Praise to him—
The Rock of my salvation.

2 Samuel 22:50, No wonder I give thanks to you, O Lord, among the nations,
And sing praises to your name.

1 Kings 8:56, Blessed be the Lord who has fulfilled his promise and given rest to his people Israel; not one word has failed of all the wonderful promises proclaimed by his servant Moses.

1 Chronicles 16:8, Oh, give thanks to the Lord and pray to him," they sang.
"Tell the peoples of the world About his mighty doings.

1 Chronicles 16:9, Sing to him; yes, sing his praises
And tell of his marvelous works.

1 Chronicles 16:34, Oh, give thanks to the Lord, for he is good;
His love and his kindness go on forever.

1 Chronicles 16:35, Cry out to him, 'Oh, save us, God of our
salvation; Bring us safely back from among the nations. Then we
will thank your holy name, And triumph in your praise.

1 Chronicles 16:36, Blessed be Jehovah, God of Israel, Forever
and forevermore, And all the people shouted "Amen!" and
praised the Lord.

1 Chronicles 23:30, Each morning and evening they stood before
the Lord to sing thanks and praise to him.

1 Peter 1:3, All honor to God, the God and Father of our Lord
Jesus Christ; for it is his boundless mercy that has given us the
privilege of being born again so that we are now members of
God's own family. Now we live in the hope of eternal life
because Christ rose again from the dead.

Revelation 5:13, And then I heard everyone in heaven and earth,
and from the dead beneath the earth and in the sea, exclaiming,
"The blessing and the honor and the glory and the power belong
to the one sitting on the throne, and to the Lamb forever and
ever."

Revelation 7:12, Amen!" they said. "Blessing, and glory, and
wisdom, and thanksgiving, and honor, and power, and might, be
to our God forever and forever. Amen!"

Revelation 19:1, After this I heard the shouting of a vast crowd in heaven, "Hallelujah! Praise the Lord! Salvation is from our God. Honor and authority belong to him alone;

Revelation 19:5, And out of the throne came a voice that said, "Praise our God, all you his servants, small and great, who fear him."

1 Chronicles 16:8, Oh, give thanks to the Lord and pray to him," they sang.
"Tell the peoples of the worldAbout his mighty doings.

1 Chronicles 16:9, Sing to him; yes, sing his praises And tell of his marvelous works.

1 Chronicles 16:34, Oh, give thanks to the Lord, for he is good; His love and his kindness go on forever.

1 Peter 1:7, These trials are only to test your faith, to see whether or not it is strong and pure. It is being tested as fire tests gold and purifies it—and your faith is far more precious to God than mere gold; so if your faith remains strong after being tried in the test tube of fiery trials, it will bring you much praise and glory and honor on the day of his return.

1 Peter 2:9, But you are not like that, for you have been chosen by God himself—you are priests of the King, you are holy and pure,

you are God's very own—all this so that you may show to others
how God called you out of the darkness into his wonderful light.

1 Peter 4:11, Are you called to preach? Then preach as though
God himself were speaking through you. Are you called to help
others? Do it with all the strength and energy that God supplies so
that God will be glorified through Jesus Christ—to him be glory
and power forever and ever. Amen.

1 Peter 4:16, But it is no shame to suffer for being a Christian.
Praise God for the privilege of being in Christ's family and being
called by his wonderful name!

Jude 24-25, And now—all glory to him who alone is God, who
saves us through Jesus Christ our Lord; yes, splendor and
majesty, all power and authority are his from the beginning; his
they are and his they evermore shall be. And he is able to keep
you from slipping and falling away, and to bring you, sinless and
perfect, into his glorious presence with mighty shouts of
everlasting joy. Amen.

Revelation 5:12, The Lamb is worthy (loudly they sang it!), the
Lamb who was slain. He is worthy to receive the power, and the
riches, and the wisdom, and the strength, and the honor, and the
glory, and the blessing."

Made in Denmark.
By Zion, The City of God

20. November 2020